EAST OF EDEN,
WEST OF ASTOR STREET

Poems of the Andrew Cunanan
Killing Spree

John David Thompson

CONTACT POET @
statepoetpro@yahoo.com

EAST OF EDEN, WEST OF ASTOR STREET
Poems of the Andrew Cunanan Killing Spree

ISBN (10-digit): 0972071776

ISBN (13-digit): 9780972071772

LIBRARY OF CONGRESS CONTROL NUMBER: 2017910829

Graphic Artwork and Electronic Layout by Karisa Runkel

MANUFACTURED IN THE UNITED STATES OF AMERICA

PALINDROME PUBLISHING OF IOWA

TO CONTACT POET: e-mail—statepoetpro@yahoo.com

Acknowledgments / Notes on Title

No poems have appeared in publication.

On Saturday, May 3, 1997, serial/spree killer Andrew Cunanan tortured and killed Chicago real estate tycoon Lee Miglin in a detached garage behind and across the alley of Miglin's Gold Coast row home. The upscale residence itself is located just west of Astor Street, one of the most affluent and distinctive neighborhoods in the entire Midwest. For years, Chicago police and the Miglin family have maintained that the murder was random so that Cunanan could switch vehicles and further distance himself from homicides he committed in Minnesota. Years later, documents released to the Chicago press indicate that Cunanan and Miglin may have known each other, thus explaining the murderer's repeated aggression against the victim and his comfort-seeming presence in the Miglin household following the violence, thus raising further questions about closet homosexuality and the pin-pulling nexus between repression and rage.

East of Eden, West of Astor Street: Poems of the Andrew Cunanan Killing Spree is a creative language arts form and offering, not a strict interpretation regarding the events.

TABLE OF CONTENTS
EAST OF EDEN, WEST OF ASTOR STREET
Poems of the Andrew Cunanan Killing Spree

CONTENT

THE QUOTABLE CUNANAN—APRES MOI, LE DELUGE

An ascendant descendant of de Leon,
I was born the fountain eternal,
a youthful spring—
my boyish eyes of chip mahogany

      mesmerizing,
                almond-flashing—

destined to be any daddy's   only dream

until generous shores swelled to fill
damned beach sands of time,
                   shifting climes
my chimes,
my climbs   tolling, trolling—
                    dethroned-down.
Mirror, tell me that I'm pretty…
Millionaire, tell me that you love me…

My wannabe wits, craven soul design to know.

My fate, my fee—a killing spree
Brilliant disguises blend into the dark corners, hungry places.

What the fuck—I deconstruct,
Tear my own playhouse down—
The dead-carpet treatment to Trail, lakeside bullets to Madson
Lexus mincemeat to Miglin, irony of fresh death in a cemetery
then diver-down to Florida flesh and fashion—in garden-tool truck, incognito, I go.

I, a foundered spout, scarcely-living doll, once heralded as handsome…
Vain Vesuvius erupts a bloodbath
               upon the gates of Versace's mansion

A flood of flowers and FBI agents commence to flow—

It is my reign; it is terror's time. Who is content with just one crime?
One-man cult of one-night stands— Man kills time; time buries man.

Murder to the Fifth Movement, I am orchestrator and master—
      Drenched in self-inflicted death, my own behest—
King Louis XV spoke it best,
                    After me, disaster.

BOOK ONE: I HAVE A GRUDGE

I HAVE A GRUDGE

I have an old bone to pick—
an enmity, a grievance, a pique, and a peeve.
Consider this my march
on San Diego, Minneapolis, the Gold Coast, South Jersey,
and, of course, Miami Beach.

The nameless become famous
before I take coarse leave of friendships, a town car, rented rooms,
and, along course, fashion's most ostensible sleeve.

Lone island, I cannot drift in retreat.

Among the vast ocean of material prosperity,
I collect myself   alone.

Whitmanesque—I siege America!
The media bites; I seize its byte-breath.

A maddening sail across state borders—
Drop-jaw clerk, can you cash this itinerant check?

(Did I mention, has my chorus mentioned
the collection of castaway bones?)

From the dune-hills of La Jolla
to the sangria stones of the Great Designed One, undone,

I have a grudge.
It carries what I must pay forward.

And I will follow.

I will come.

SAN DIEGO ZOO

Men are animals.
You can fuck or fuck with the gay ones at Hillcrest,
the alternative San Diego Zoo.

Andrew Cunanan is the quintessential zoo user,
a keeper of damaged souls in soulless cages.

Under the working pseudonym of Andrew DeSilva,
he feeds the bottom fish and top mammals
lines of fodder…claiming to be an heir, an owner.

Their militant attention is a beach.
His stories, the comber.

See them all in high season at Rich's or Flicks,
whispering about crystal meth and talking with their dicks.

Look at Cunanan clawing and pawing his way
among preferential cliques, in-crowd groups.

He is a ringmaster with a big ring.
Watch them all jump through hoops.

One night he is walking alone,
the next ambling in jet-set packs—
maintaining flawless zoo records of those
bare-backing behind each other's backs.

The martinis are dry; the juice behind them is dish-wet.

Behind, between, and inside these bars

the only thing running higher than beastly, about-me fever,

credit-card debt.

BEACHED BABY

Gaining gravity, sinking in Nocturne's sift,

I lift my ear to the conch-gypsy,

And she speaks, she speaks in basin waves.

Her seaweed beads tell in echo-shell,

You salt-rimmed, foundered flesh,

You vine-battered whore,

You cannot discover breaching oceans

Until you lose sight of the long-tooth shore.

A KIND OF CIVIL DISOBEDIENCE

A crowd of one

forms around a piping fuel.

Both simmer like cayenne in creole

beneath a bowling sky.

Speaker, witness, interpreter—a spoon of the same soup.

The soul stands on a soapbox,

steams a self-petition to the mind.

A recipe for revenge seethes through open artery-air:

these cheese rinds, bloody greens—recipe list of black grievances.

Private and violent, an ingénue entremetier stirs, folds, and bends

Thoreau's cookbook of rules.

SOAPBOX

You could make a derby car out of that soapbox, boy—race yourself out of town.

Like mounting a corpulent Florentian woman
At the Renaissance orgy,
You get up on it.

Speak. Bellow. Proclaim.
Clouds from your self-conversation
Clutter like fist crumps of paper.

The insouciant canter by.

In convivial daylight, it course-rains.

This is interior lecture,
Makeshift theater, swarm-gathering of one.

The crate is a crave in the soul.

What won't dismiss from those discharged lips,
You elocute with iron tools

And a gun.

TIDE AND PRIME

Let us go, you and I—
Where the tide subsides
Where memories are dream wet
But the sand…abandoned-castled…dry.

We could go there alone
Where the shells are exposed
Where they align for a kind of chiropractic exam
To set their set bones.

Let us take our bald feet
Where passion's polyps recede
Where we walk on Nautilus crust
Like stepping stones.

Let us make our hearts' pace
Lay our remains among the combed waste
Salute our last shines
Toward the retreating foam.

CALIFORNIA SCHEMING

The Golden State is known for its quakes,
dirt-born tempests that give Richter a quiver.

California is also renowned for its glorious boys,
resplendent sandstorm creatures
with Malibu flexes and come-hither features—

and one, in peculiar,
about to lose his Midas thrust,
such precarious bliss
dethroned from the A-list
to a pauper's bust.

Accustomed to penthouses,
he must acclimate to ditches.

His mind splits to a fault
in the voices of frenetic witches.

The remains of his brain is a cauldron.
It toils a black brew.

It boils to trouble.

Pops won't lick his chops.

Moneyed dandies no longer find his pus charming.
The mirror no longer reflects fair.
At last, he no longer stands crotch-to-crotch
with the incoming twenty-one somethings,
calientes from Caracas,
the ones with designer pubic hair.

The moment foments to a rendering,
only a spree of reckonings will undo.

He lifts off—a wicked-west suffragette,
green-thighed, vengeance-eyed
straddled upon a Northwest Airline jet—

traffic controllers, at first, mistake for a broom.

SYBARITE

Before the three-month spree,
there is Easy Street—
its lamp-lit pursuits,
but, alas, none of its inner-circle permanence.

A transient sashay,
profit and comfort's parade—
glide, swagger, and sway—
drop a line of crystal, sham inheritance,

or a foreign name,

a loner like you can trust on getting laid.

In fact, you can bank on it.

Peddle chiseled wares.
Pitch an uptown, hideaway tent.

The older gents pay a mindful to you—
and your rent.

Bon vivant! Bon viveur!
You're French in a pinch,
a hedonist at scant heart
beating on desperate doorsteps
for an American host.

You contour your dubious personalities
to cater to the aging whim on leather stool.

Cunanan. DeSilva. Morales. Whoever.

You take him for money, sport, and a fool.

You'd suck the sand from the coast
if you thought it would render a pitcher of paradise.

If only the barkeep would spill a little cider vinegar in your glass…
to rid the establishment of such a coming-of-age

parasite.

THRIFTY DRUG STORE COWBOY

Among the scripts of bottled lies
Cunanan measured, packaged, and doled out
to the burning ears on the barstools of Hillcrest,
this was one of omission or mistaken identity.

He never clerked at Thrifty Drug Store.

To speak of it was to speak social evil.

The bespectacled counter jockey,
the jerk behind the soda jerks—
whoever he was—a mere semblance
of Andrew who was filming on location in Mexico
at the time, any time,
a regular job, a daily wage mentioned
on the privileged lips sipping Sunday mimosas.

Salary of shame, grapevine dive
to admit, confess
he was hustling bandages,
pimping scoops of pralines and cream
to the Rancho Bernardo cliché-clientele
from nine to five.

THE RED SCARE

Andrew believed in a lot of things—
He deserved to be rich.
He was destined to be famous.
He had tested positive for HIV / AIDS.

Among these conjectures, the latter became obsession.
Too chicken shit to read or receive the results,
Cunanan insisted on the atrocious and began exhibiting
A false pregnancy of symptoms—
Panic rash, sweats in the sheets, dry heaves in the mouth.

His friends were no longer loyal to him with their pocketbooks.
Could it be a scant of those scags had been disloyal to him with their penises—
Infecting the kept cutie in his prime, their deranged cocks culpable for his demise?

Cunanan's immune system was intact, yet his belief system unraveled;
The uninformed mind firmly made.

And so his routine cruise wheeled into historic crusade.
Reasonable interrogation waned to hysterical, self-indulgent suspicion.

He formed a one-man committee,
Purchased a one-way ticket to tirade,
Battered the hapless, healthy and hung with a hammer and gun—
Sending bones home to good-die-young graves.

Some rant. Some friend.

And if you were caught in his running mascara line of fire,

Well, you'd never breathe in this town again.

ODE TO BOY TOY

You are the warmer weather—
        of May-December,

                moony-eyed, celestial light
to the right
        of a gray, dimming side.

All about you appears brighter—
milk-and-saucer teeth, flawless smile—
        kinks that couldn't be blonder,
starving jeans that this eye-candy evening,
        could not be bone-tighter.

But the Michael Kors strap on your wrist,
        It taunts and it ticks.
As you pause and pose for the sugar paparazzi,
        It declines to stand still.
Yes, It declines and declines—
        and soon,
                        you will.

Yet, Spring still sports on the branch.
It remains within shrinking minutes
                        of the trophy hour.
Muster what luster you can—
                pick, pan, and scour.

They will be calling you an unattached man soon,
        and that's not booming news
        to you, cash-strapped son,

who will be turned out like a vagabond cat
        around midnight
                        when you turn twenty-one.

A POISON GLEE

After William Blake's A Poison Tree

I came across a poison glee
A liar in the choir
Vocally corded in hypocrisy

A cunning castrato
Restrained, repressed
In prepubescent immaturity

A borrower of notes
A stealer of song
A tainter of chambers

Who honed the grudge tone long….

We were quarrelsome chaps
Belting our pitches
Along Bishop's privileged halls.

I prayed for his voice
To drop the indecencies

But he hadn't the balls.

HELLO, YELLOW BRICK ROAD

If Cunanan were that gold-digging cur

in the Elton John/Bernie Taupin song,

he would have affixed his soul,

every piece of luggage his Hillcrest ass owned

to that gilded street of ease,

those bricks of old-coin yellow.

Prince Andrew's inherited air would never land.

The stock up his derriere would never come down.

He'd be a metaphorical whore,

if only Uncle Henry would open the treasure door.

Akin to an indoor ficus,

you can plant him, daddy, in your penthouse.

Cunanan would be a long-term bond, you can hold forever.

Where's the privileged pen to sign up for you?

Wrap him up, gigolo-to-go, in Spandex and hose,

a present for your rich clique to open.

He'll account to the account-abled

wearing nothing but a lollipop from the all-boy guild—

and a chap-tapping pair of ruby shoes.

SNIFFING FOR TICKETS OR TIDBITS

It is the morning of the mongrels.

They come by bus.

>They dislodge themselves
>from trench-coat-logged trains.

With low-jawed sense of esteem,
>with heightened sense of smell,

they search the narrow streets
for a morsel of city swells.

Easy onto Easy Street will require a ticket,
an admit, a wink-wag, a pass.

Fresh out of fat wallets,
their ambition ambulates,
walk the walk,
paws on front glass.

So, how much for that lonely millionaire
in Starbuck's window,
the one with Centurion American Express?

A steam press of the pelvic nose,
Fortune's wind blows.

It's a cash bar inside his car.

And you're both biscuit and guest.

NARCISSISM

Remove the Greek allusion,
all theatrical or diagnostic terminology—

strip its petal bare,

and you are footed in a pool of self-pity.

The world of compare-and-contrast
conquers you at last.

Lean into its water with a wishing stick,

reflect, gently bend—

and you'll discover just beyond its breaking edges,

you've received

the short end.

JEALOUSY AND ENVY

The distinction is delicate,
a subtle difference
between threat of loss
and the acquisitive want of desire.

Both emotions appear to be triggered
by the material, the physical
what we have, see, and covet—

the foaming of the mind
when we've had enough of this world,
and at the same time,
cannot extract enough from it.

Jealousy and envy were the impassioned
travel companions of Andrew Cunanan,
his own virtual Thelma and Louise,
perched on each shoulder
urging one murder to convert
into a spree.

Jealousy had convinced him
Jeffrey and David were behind-his-back together,
keeping each other's hearts warm
in the relentless Minnesota leather-weather.

Envy was less delusional, yet more shallow
reminding Andrew of his residency in Loserville
while those about him located themselves
in cities of cash, status, and careers.

Both were putting the weight on him and tabbing the years.

Fanatical co-pilots, impulsive backseat drivers—
and, to borrow a cliché' from the gays, a couple of vicious queens—

imposing their selfish, emotive ways
even during the Gold Coast getaway
when Andrew spun out of town in a Lexus
the shade of their collective complexion, green.

SOCIOPATH

You could put the *path* in sociopath.

Through measured leaves, you heed

A trodden black,

A road sparse-travelled by reputable jacks.

You seek out the grassy, the gullible

In want of your wear, etiology of ruin.

You summon your soulless character

For quiet, calculated attack,

Birth of the bruise.

Your craft picks the woods clean.

All is shadowlands

Sighing ages and ages, hence, bare.

The cold trail you blaze deviates,

Diverges into imperceptible simmer and sin.

Suspicion blinks, but never quite brightens.

A gaslight dims.

THE GAY RAGES

Like grief,
it occurs in stages.

At first,
a tepid inclination,

toward a socioeconomic injustice,
or denial

of the wrinkle in time
pressing as one ages.

It begins to boil
beneath the first bald spot,

then simmers beyond
the initial hissy-fit.

It bargains with no one,
not even the id.

It is a raving baby,
though it's nobody's kid.

Then it snaps
like a faggot in an agitated fireplace.

She-devil, promiscuous in hot pink,
it starts spreading the bad news—

you're leaving today.

And to depress you into acceptance,
a pink pistol in your face.

RICH OVER TROUBLED WATER

It is said—
A drowning man takes down
Those nearest to him.

Martha proclaimed it
Between brandies and brays
In *Who's Afraid of Virginia Woolf?*

To know Andrew Cunanan was to stroke with him—
His ego or a bantering joke—whatever kept the social season afloat.

Speaking of kept, America's Most Dauntless wrote the manual on it.

Before he had sunk his last nickel—
And a claw hammer into the skull of a trusting friend,
Andrew was sinking between Sans Diego and Francisco.
La Jolla itself had become La Joyless.

Cunanan had ingratiated himself with the toast of the Gay West Coast,
Seeking out, not so much lifebuoys,
But flush daddies to support his extravagant, submerging sail.

To know him was to pay for him.
But lately—it was like putting toothpaste back in a tube—
Andrew and his silver-haired hectics
All standing around the hourglass of drifting ruby-red sands
Like a bunch of time-surrendered Dorothys.

The gay old gentry of California better be good and accustomed
To breathing heavily upon glass—
Soon, their rarefied noses will be glued to the set and screen
Doggish pants of anxiety
With Andrew emerging as a five o'clock shadow
On the national evening news.
Is he coming next for me? Is he brooding next for you?

Count eccentric Norman Blachford in that goose-bumped group, for one.
But why drop names
When both feet are three, four-feet and descending into the grave?

GOODBYE TO YOU

You're going away.
Shall we bake you a cake?
At least let us boys about to disband
Chip in to spring for a dismissive dessert.

The drinks stiffen low in the glass.
Let's raise those spirits on your behalf.
Their crystal clang is the social rub
You can feel when our eyes collectively smile,
Then slyly avert.

You're leaving sour and strapped with no forwarding address.
Parting is sweet bliss, for most of us, no less.

Rumor has it—
Your wallet is runway model thin,
So is your stash of menagerie, antique men
Whose bitter-boned emotions close the curio door
To prepare for a new token-tod boy
They will shelve at the next retreat of Gamma Mu.

My God! You were the proverbial glue holding and binding us queens.
How subtle, yet bitter this farewell dinner at California Cuisine.

Even your favorite waiter writes you off, the final course
In a kind of unkind raspberry puree calligraphy
Caressing the plate of your chocolate truffle tort.

Your salutary guests can almost taste it—
The curt and cold message ostensibly omitting
Your name, Andrew.

Such callous, salivating words
Disguised in the art of confectionary curves:

Goodbye to You

BOOK TWO: SPREE AT LAST, SPREE AT LAST

SPREE AT LAST, SPREE AT LAST

Andrew Cunanan had a dream.

He wanted to be somebody.
He yearned for wealth.

He refused to work the requisite hours
to stir such a dream into reality's waking.

His post-adolescent years were a decade at the debutante's ball—
always a coming out, an announcement, a proclamation
to the gullible, the profitable in California's gay social circles.
He craved their collective attention.

Conniving and kept,
Andrew accrued other people's credit
until all cards and his welcome—were overextended.

His reputation fell like Frisco in the '06 earthquake.

Cunanan bolted from the bay and its chains in a tempest
of vengeance and fury.

He headed east, you could say, to cash a check,
an emotion, a sense that held him manacled to inferiority's debt.

Those who had surpassed him on the ladder,
those who had found true love—
lay to rest as fresh victims along his binge of blood.

Wheeling down freeways in a cloud of the stolen—
vehicles, identities, and a gun,
Andrew exercised his civil blight upon selected geographies.

He had a dream. He had a dream…

                              the aging daylight would not let him keep,

enslaved by greed's rage,
taking himself for a most joyless ride, a most hapless spree.

PHEROMONE

From Ancient Greece,
it is what we bear forward.

It is what the foreshadowed reek.

Like a phantom bullet,
it emits from spit-body…
all impetus and mist.

It opens, extends receiving organs
with scant scent of a sable-scythe kiss.

Such incensed seduction, tempered alarm,
Its spy-ice hubris
                    scatters a trail of lascivious crumbs.

Indeed, it seeps, then it feeds before it disarms.

Mariner-caller, it finger-lingers
each weathered merchant, each moon-smitten sailor home.

It summons Aphrodite to rise from brewed tides,
stake her nude heart into its tint-tethered paradise

above the sea-foam.

BROTHER ANDREW'S TRAVELLING SALVATION SHOW

Superman plans on being a bad boy.
And soon, he will be grounded
to the wheels that carry lowly mortals away.

But for now,
he is a bird in a plane,
the S of sadomasochistic sin on his chest,
leaping from Silicon Beach
                    to the North Star plain
        over the rage of the Rockies
in a single bound.

Again, he elevates. Again, he ascends
        on someone else's wings
with travel bags of testosterone, crystal meth, and fear.

The social butterfly alights on a thawing Metropolis,
        ignites crime,
rolls one victim in his red cape.
His gun of steel leaves another, ex-lover, along a cryptic shore.

His sub-heroic actions headline *The Daily Planet*.
The skies are closed from Smallville to Krypton,
        but the roads are open—
He seizes a red Jeep Cherokee, rolls into the Windy City,
        makes a notorious nexus with a Gold Coast captain,
commandeers the tortured tycoon's Lexus—jet sets away.

Not so much a manhunt—as a punkhunt—is APB'd on him.
The fabulous fugitive of Astor Street joyrides until he is a brief Jersey boy,
kills in a cemetery, then trucks down Interstate 95, grave maker in disguise.

The poster child of America's Most Wanted, he morphs into kind of folk villain,
his own finder and keeper, charismatic chameleon, spreading a sermon of revenge—
        the gospel according to an old gigolo, testament of gore.

Brother Love won't make it to a hot August night—and for that—
the gay men's choir in San Diego sings a collective, *Halle-Halle-lu-jah!*
No, he won't ride into August—but he hides about houseboats in Miami—
        where he sees a ragged tent, beachfront villa of Versace—
pitches his signature pistol,
                    puts fashion and the FBI on the floor.

DECLARATION OF DEPENDENCE

If Andrew Cunanan was not the Anti-Christ,
He was the anti-Thomas Jefferson.

His reliance on the kindness of elders
Bound him to be the Blanche DuBois of the Greater San Diego Area.

Dependent as a newborn, wanton as a Southern belle-whore,
Andrew's lies were self-evident brutes, ubiquitous even to the blindest of backers.

When in the intercourse of human events,
Cunanan knew that not all bank accounts were created equal—

And to tap into the fortuity of a trust fund,
One first must gain, well, trust.

Andrew used ingratiation to pursue Life, Liberty, Happiness—
To flatter and attract, truckle and charm.

Cunanan had it made by making himself at home,
Fixing himself a drink.

This became his signature declare,
Written with dubious ink.

NORHTERN LIGHTS

When the anger won't thaw,
you head for the northern lights
where the moose is and are
known to let off a little snout-steam.

The northern lights,
like Andrew's fury senses,
peptic, enlightened little devils,
gaseous collisions
claiming headward turf.

Intuition suggested to him—
it seemed more than mere coincidence—
an ex-lover and recent object affection—
David Madson and Jeffrey Trail—
just so happened, that's right, just so happened
to both up and leave southern California
for the city that made fictive Mary Richards a producer
and Mary Tyler Moore breathtakingly famous.

Speaking of Marys,
Cunanan had a brutal hockey score
to settle with those two conniving queers.

Reassurance on the long-distance wire
that nothing, nothing
but a platonic connection had developed between them
did not subside his suspicious mind.

Disembarking onto the freeze-seething sub-arctic
of manifest Minnesota,
even Andrew's pea-green demeanor could not ignore
the Borealis of an awakening April sky,
its heaven-hither blue.

He rolled up his duffel bag and sleeves,
talked both patsies into giving weekend house keys—

you see—

Miss Mary is not the only girl about town
who can produce the news.

A TALE OF TWIN CITIES

I.

Before Chicago,
long before the sand reaches of Miami,
an angry Andrew managed to muster
a one-way ticket to Minneapolis-St. Paul.

He had begun to depersonalize people, friends—
telling dinner guests at the last supper in California:
He had *business* to settle in the Midwest.

That business was a Naval Academy graduate, Jeffrey Trail
and a former lover, architect David Madson.

Andrew appeared to be the obtuse-angle out
of some type of quasi-love triangle.

Who owed whom money—
Who owed whom an apology, explanation, or anything
remains a conundrum to even the most interior of insiders.

Neither Jeffrey nor David wanted Andrew there.
By late April 1997,
nobody wanted Andrew Cunanan/DeSilva anywhere.

The frost breaks late in Minnesota.
It can hold its wintry hazes like a selfish grudge.

After clawing his way into the lives of the homosexual elite,
Cunanan took a claw hammer
to Jeffrey Trail's skull on Sunday night—in Madson's borrowed loft.

Trail had told friends he would meet them later at the Gay Nineties.

He wouldn't even make it to his Gay Thirties.

A Tale of Twin Cities

II.

The who, what, and whereabouts of David Madson
the days following his lover's death
appear as unbalanced and unclear
as Andrew Cunanan's unraveled mind.

He was sighted with another man—
                    walking a dog on a leash—
or was Madson the dog on the leash?

Fear is a sort of trance if it cannot be fully expressed.

Madson was an early suspect in his lover's demise.
After all, the body was rolled in a carpet in David's loft
amidst sexual and drug paraphernalia.

Andrew and David were living, breathing—and gone, baby, gone.

Most of us like to think of David as an unassuming hostage for days—
a hostage who knew too much.

And just where outside of Murderapolis had Cunanan and tacit captive gone?

Andrew Wyeth, the famed naturalist painter, could have immortalized the landscape here—
East Rush Lake, an hour north of the Twin Cities—
the water thawing for sportsmen—the water in David's decomposing eye thawing for clues.

Instead, Andrew Cunanan created another murderous masterpiece—lakeside—
extracting blood and trust from his field companion.

The words *serial* and *spree* just beginning to gather like bullet dust
on the tips of journalists' pens, the American tongue.

Shoreline is time—
Andrew and the state of Minnesota possess more
than Illinois, New Jersey,
Florida, and California…combined.

IF YOU CAN KILL YOUR GOOD FRIENDS

You can best anyone.

Such was the conditional thought,
initial premise shivering down the spines
of anyone inclined to recall
a rendezvous, an acquaintance of any kind
with Andrew Cunanan or Andrew DeSilva.

The surfers and Seals in San Diego
gathered in a weathered cloud of uncertain fear—

reminisced him a buddy, an –ex, or a queer.

As far as paranoia goes and grows,
this is as hissy-fit as it gets—
afraid to go out, afraid to stay in—
questions about associations with Andrew
the most popular gossip-topic among the company of questionable men.

Did I screw him over?
Was I a bad lay?
I just tested positive…wonder if I gave him AIDS?

The S & M greased and diseased down on their knees,
a vicious-suspicious circle prepared for a good knighting.

Those who had secret carnal disposal of Cunanan
swallow their own vomit like intestinal semen in a closet,

for where do you hide when you're already hiding?

MIDWEST SIDE STORY

He had taken a jet,
then morphed into a sort
of Great Plains shark—

seizing wheels,
claiming temporary turf.

In a *Midwest Side Story*
port of way,
it's the off-Broadway
stage-and-slay musical play
Jerome Robbins
forgot to choreograph.

Pause for applause or ironic laugh.
Cunanan's intermission is their finale.
It's all for criminal charity, the bedeviled's behalf.

Jeffrey is downstage, wrapped in blood-red carpet.
David is all in cords, vocals pleading for Andrew to stop it.
Lee waits in a garage pit,
where the tell-orchestra warms its gardening strings.

Friends left for forensics, the wanted on wing—

These are a few of Andrew's favorite things.

But why all the opulent, Americanized vehicular fuss?
A Jeep Cherokee? A Lexus?
Miss Cunanan is lucky getting away here.

He'd feel prettier if the felon were to follow script,
change into a Puerto Rican in a phone booth
ready to rumble on the South Side of Chicago…

steal himself a mighty, right fine Gran Torino.

Hell, put a Betty Rubble wig, revival heels on that wanted man….

Chameleon in a corset,
say hello in the rearview mirror
to Rita Moreno.

THE CHICAGO SKYLINE

The high-art horizon of architecture,
it cuts scalene and sharp,
a graduate of its own Chicago School.

Birthplace of
vertical steel,
it rises from
bucket fire and
flame water
to roof a jag-
ged House of Blues.

This is where Sullivan teams with Sandburg,
Big-Shouldered
in its words and its wires,
outlining the corpse of the living, the pulsating.

Storied and towered,
it vests a limitless vista,
fields a freight
of colossal columns,
shapes the otherwise flat-starred prairie
to a dimensional sphere.

It opens
like a gleaming dark rosebush,
as the work-hour closes,
yes, opens into the gasping chest,
breath-taken heart of the Midwest,

opens and opens

like a pruning pair of garden shears.

THE BULLS AND THE BEARS

A lakefront city
with champion-ringed teams
named for beasts on the market of trade,
Chicago sports its own horns,
swipes a thrashing claw down
at any competitor that dares to confront it.

There are no vigils here,
for you cannot hold a candle to it—
at least, not in the nation's heart.

Tycoons and their storied walls
create their own arenas,
wake in a wilderness of investment's design.

No matador, no trap—
ever to deter its upwardly mobile
hoof-and-print path.

STAR BUCK

Once Andrew Cunanan and his killing-spree machine
wheeled into the Greater Chicago area,
rumor and legend have it
that he spent hours brewing his next lethal scheme
at a Greek coffee shop on Division and State.

Almond-eyed and hybrid ethnic,
this pigmented prince virtually slipped by
the memory of each peripatetic passer-by
who took him at the time, more or less,
as a nobody.

Andrew wanted to be a somebody.

He blended in well enough
like skim milk over bitter espresso,
furtively steaming,
surreptitiously foaming,
downing cup after cup,
refilling his cowardice courage,
swallowing any last vestige of sense or compassion,
and, of course, leaving little or no tip.

After a double-shot in Minneapolis,
he is caffeine-recharged,
heartless and hard,
prepared for a single-shot
once Marilyn heads out of town—Toronto bound,
and his man Miglin is left tinkering, alone,
in an unattached garage.

FABULOUS ASTOR STREET

Nobody walks here. Nothing wheels.

In resplendent synchronicity,
all genteel mobility—everything strolls.

Sunlight drops jackpot coins
though a greenback reach of blue-blooded trees
above Doric columns and floral motifs.

Authority should ban all tread and feet,
mandate the made-in-the-shade esplanade
to nothing but carriage and horse—

barouche, Victoria, or chaise hoof-gliders
that drift like lilac-winded lifts
through destiny's course.

What better place to digress,
invest an alien element
to, momentarily, take the rarefied down—

those petrified-posed, sullied one Sunday dawning...
all bantering and cantering,
the talk and gossip-trot of the town.

ON THE STREET WHERE YOU LIVE

Avenue of dandies
adorned with Laura Ashley families.

Enchantment creeps from porch corridors
like moonlit hydrangeas.

The sun-and-shade of money in bloom,
each bulb a gushing debutante.

It is spring on the street where you live.

A soft rain has cleaned the paves
for the gentry's walking.

Children chase pastel playmates
to the tides of North Lake Shore.

Here, you discover the color of wonder,
the magnificence, munificence of success and season
unfolding, unwrapping for best lens of summer.

The panorama breaks of a commoner's gaze
in tints of egg custard, lavender, and cresson.

God himself is Professor Higgins,
giving neighborhood birds advanced voice lessons.

MY FAIR MIGLIN

Is it wrong to presume
that he is an upper-crust Pygmalion
carving the boy-beasts from the streets
to emerge a more eclectic, statuesque ilk
for himself and such well-heeled clientele?

And just who
is giving oral lessons to whom—
the articulate spectacular,
phonetic feeding between one have and one have-not,
a couple of ne'er-do-well swells in Eden's other lot?

It is early May.
One must profess a reign of terror falls mainly on the plain.
In this tragedy of bad manners,
who will command the appropriate language
to effect all to a halt?

Some rendezvous. Some weekend retreat.
My fair Miglin is dead meat.
But, at least, it has ceased raining.
The only thunder is the gas of the family Lexus leaving.
The only drizzle, the speechless sprinking of last rites

and garage-floor salts.

CAT'S AWAY

Mice are like unattended children.
They create their own devil-may-care worlds
if the prudent rodents think
no one is looking.

Their sensitive whiskers
prefer homes with imperceptible cracks,
leaks and slits
that lead way to fantasy and feeding

after accepted fact.

And the play. They play—
like a Disney charade.

It's a film. Four syllables.
Sounds like *it grows, it grows*.

I've got it on the tip of my throat—*Pinocchio!*

This boy lies. This boy lies.
Why, he is the farmhouse wife himself

with a keen butcher knife.

The cat may make it back
from Canada in cosmetic tact,

but that is one gnash in the garage
who won't make it out alive

from his own self-imposed trap.

I FALL TO PIECES

The figurative sense of the phrase,
its imaginative idiom,
must precede the more literal intent
when examining
the Cunanan-Miglin affair.

Neither Humpty Dumpty
nor Patsy Cline's crooning
could put poor Andrew together again
once he'd snapped the tether
and rolled like an emotional wrecking ball
throughout the Upper Midwest.

He died a worse death than Christ,
Anna Miglin, Lee's mother, told Chicago papers.

The autopsy, the anatomy of her son's remains
spilling the gut-gory details
of a murder and murderer
who seemed to take sport in torture.

Pick a body part any body part.
Miglin's demolished chassis ends where it begins where it ends.
His entire frame wrapped in duct tape
with space left in the nose for breathing—
a plastic bag ceremoniously draped over his dead head.

Lee Miglin had become the potted plant
for *Sadomasochistic Homes and Gardens.*

Throat slit by garden bow saw,
his chest had more pruning punctures and holes in it
than the grand stories Cunanan used to tell
the in-crowd clientele around Hillcrest in San Diego.

When the dismemberment of his dignity and sum parts were done,
Lee became in-garage road kill, a victim of his own Lexus' hit-and-run.

THE GOLDILOCKS OF GORE

Papa Bear is still at home,
but this does not daunt
the Goldilocks of Gore
from bloodletting herself
into the Miglin quarters—

in-your-face occupancy,
brutish intrusion—
a sinister type of bed, bath, and beyond.

Throughout the estate,
she stakes her claim—
a spoon sticking out of a pint of Haagen-Dazs,
a knife perpendicular to a plateless slab of ham.

This is her territory now.

Pestilent, unwanted guest—
helps herself to cola and clothes,
even removes some tell-tale facial stubble
in her tenancy of trouble—
keeping a madhouse, and the family dog, Honey
under her thumb.

She moves through rooms
that once-upon-a-time belonged to a real-estate tycoon,
leaving open doors and clues behind
like a buffet of bread crumbs.

THE 1997 KENTUCKY DERBY

It is brutally ironic,
or perhaps queerly coincidental,
that the same day,
the duplicate afternoon
Andrew Cunanan tortured and slayed Lee Miglin,
the 123rd *Running of the Roses* entered horse history
at Churchill Downs.

The winner was *Silver Charm*.
To place, *Captain Bodgit*.
And to show, *Free House*.

Cunanan maintained a sort of silver charm about him,
a somewhat second-rate panache
that often passed for first class
if one were desperate or foolish.

Captain Bodgit, of course, was Miglin himself.
In Britain, *to bodge* is to do a clumsy, inelegant job.
Whether tinkering with his Bitter or Lexus,
or scheduling a same-sex, clandestine rendezvous,
Miglin dead-meat messed up,
if and when granting Cunanan to the gate
that overcast afternoon.

And to show? A free house.
After all, Marilyn was out-of-country, out of town.
Andrew made himself a sandwich and a serial killer
inside the Miglin double townhouse—
while Lee was on all-fours, put down—
strewn like losing race tickets about the garage floor.

When Marilyn came home from Canada,
the Sunday socialite lost by a nose—
nothing but death's perfume,
a scent of scandal
to welcome her at the door.

IT HAPPENS EVERY MAY

The seasoned
pole is
garland-wreathed,
flower-fit
for the taut
weave travel.

It takes just
one child,
out of step,
and into scheme

       for it all
          to unravel.

POST MORTEM MIGLIN

After the Rocky Horror Garden Show,

early reports from the SUN-TIMES indicated

the Miglin Lexus had become more like a Rolls,

arrhythmically trampling and tread-mowing

over Lee's corpse.

But for an in-house demolition derby,

the crime port appeared rather clean,

mere trifles of splattering, relatively blood-free.

Mr. Miglin himself, fully-dressed,

tan suede jacket, white tab-collar shirt

buttoned to the nines;

yet beneath this textile surface,

pooled wounds to the heart

deep enough for an irretrievable dive.

Head bagged in plastic and paper,

tag-team cement sacks to the chest,

breaking each of the victim's ribs,

turning the Gold Coast tycoon to mush—

whatever the killer's obsession, infatuation,

it ended with a resounding crush.

BLUE MARILYN

It is both a drink
and a socialite wife—
left in the morning-light dark,
intoxicated with terror,
just a slip of the lip
from sobriety
during this most enduring Sunday brunch.

Unsunny Came Home

It is the mood of the feast-
your-numb eyes upon this,

a foul-play flavor
you offer to forthcoming neighbors
gathered in bleak   around back.

The despaired raise a glass,
a grim mimosa hung over from Saturday matinee mayhem.

A mere taste of the truth,
                and you've had your fill

until the proof presses to drink on, drink on....

And you will. You will.

HUSH, PUPPIES

Among other titles
ranging from narcissist to narcotics trader,
Andrew Cunanan was a cynophile, a canophile—
a connoisseur of our canine friends.

This fond familiarity with pedigree
may have enabled him
to kill in relative silence.

The attendant dogs, it seems,
were not only house-trained,
but crime-scene complicit.

Indeed, the Trail and Miglin murders
were senseless and barkless.

Prints, David Madson's dalmatian,
may have been out walking
during the nailing of Trail,
yet neighbors claim to have heard
not an utterance from the stately beast
for days while Jeffrey's body lay
rolled like a Cuban cigar Andrew was akin to smoking.

And Honey.
Honey. Honey. Honey.
The Cunanan-cat had that labrador's tongue
while owner Mr. Miglin was given the Glasgow smile,
then driven over by his own wheels of misfortune.

Andrew may have instilled bone-fear
into these creatures—
or ingratiated himself,
sent their wags to quiet corner,
put them to heel.

It's a dog-eat-dog world.
Cunanan was in the midst of devouring it.
Who were these lowly mangers to interrupt such a dog-hearted meal?

STORING HONEY

Honey, any apiarist
worth his combs will tell you,
does not muck up, spoil
if stored properly—
a dry, dark closeted area perhaps—
much like the vault
where Lee Miglin kept his formulas
of preference and privilege.

For if Honey is exposed
to moisture of any kind—
the bedew of blood spattering
along the apron of a three-vehicle garage,
for example—
it will ferment,
even seethe—
show the buzz of its teeth.

ANY LEXUS OF MINE

Jealousy thrives in the color of jade —

Andrew attacked in 1997,
the year of the locust.

He was a one-man band,
all nymph and swarm,
stripping homes, damaging families,
green in his consumption
of anything green.

17 years later—

The buzz
that had been plaguing the public,
still murmuring, ill-acquiesced—

Cunanan may have known Miglin
prior to unearthing
contents from the poor-rich man's chest.

Brazen, ostentatious—
Cunanan was out of the Butcher House
in luxury, leaving behind
catch-me-if-you-can clues as bureaucratic stings.

He boxes Lee in the garage
then jacks the Miglin jade-black wheels
to give him fresh wings.

DESPERATE ODD HO

If only the FBI had been backed up
by the vocal stylizations of Don Henley
and the nameless rest of the Eagles' nest,
perhaps our nation's top drawer—
in the federal bureau could have established
an accurate character profile of Cunanan
in an effort to decipher, uncover his freak-mystique
before one blood bash led to another.

Obese by gay standards,
obsolete to the social circles
in which he once shined in dead-center circle,
Andrew, henceforth, lived on taken time—
stolen lives, misused tools, a surrogate gun—
and, by journey's end, the across-the-border vehicles
owned by a triumvirate of his own victims.

A pauper. A robber. A first-degree knock-you-offer.
To the casual examiner, he was Cliché Cunanan—
at wit's end, the end of his rope.
Life had left him lemons in the sour taste of rejection and dope.

Yet, as redundant as his run may superficially be,
Andrew Cunanan remained an evasive enigma to pursuant authorities
who left a blind eye to the gay culture that, unwittingly, would aid and abet him
who would strike again like sulfur on a stick—lest the watching world might forget him.

Out of fashion with his Crystal City friends,
and, for God's sakes, out of California fitness—
the boy at your death's door might have been wrested in the Midwest
if only the feds had truly infiltrated "where he lived,"—
or, better yet, if Cunanan had ever left behind a living witness.

SAIL ON, DE SILVA GIRL

The phrase,
like anything or anyone
Andrew Cunanan ever possessed,
is, to say the least, borrowed.

Derivative from the third, added verse
Bridge over Troubled Water,
the coined catch became fighting words
between the dynamic duo—
Simon & Garfunkel.

Paul wrote it, reluctantly,
for the sake of Art—and his incessant harping
the ballad needed an orchestral maneuver
near its conclusion.

When applied to Andrew,
it's less Art-sy fartsy.

Sail on, DeSilva girl—
aging precipice
from an ashen peak of mediocrity
at best.

Cunanan could use an orchestra himself about now—
Strings, and better yet, a chamber—

to harbor
and "cheap hotel" his aging anger.

SCARBOROUGH FAIRY

Putting the kibosh on those close to him
transformed Andrew Cunanan
into a sort of Renaissance man with further plan.

Having slain in some of the Midwest's
most sophisticated cities,
he had evolved, become quite the cutpurse of heartbeats.

In the wake of three deaths,
Andrew experienced rebirth—an unconscionable confidence—
wheeling ever eastward, considerable distance

from considerable crimes.

Indeed, Cunanan had gone medieval on some fag asses.

His chameleon looks longed for the masked masses
to further the invoking dance with ingénue FBI.

The scarves and taverns of New York City—
its sash-dashes, bustled ruffles—

why, he might even snap a parsley of crack cocaine,
borrow advice from a passing street sage,
put his traveling rose in some Mary at Stonewall—

and buy a little minstrel time.

FOR LOVE OF THE UNION AND CONFEDERATE DEAD

The unsung victim of Cunanan's killing spree,
William Reese was the caretaker
at Finn's Point National Cemetery—New Jersey,
but caretaker is perhaps too mundane a term
to plot his occupancy,
this shepherd, this steward
dedicated to the respectful tending, and tendering
of reposed soldiers,
both Union and Confederate,
recumbent in honor's slumber, perpetual sleep.

Families arrive, here, in unannounced intervals
looking for ancestors, traces to the past,
links to history, its heroics and tragedy.

Andrew Cunanan arrived looking for wheels.
Thug found 'em.

Functional homicide—criminologists call it,
nothing personal.

The caretaker's quarters is a house of stone
and remote light.

Evil seeks this kind of solitary refinement
on a whim—or on its own calculating terms.

Andrew needed to dump the Lexus like a bad date—
or routine fuck.

Before his avarice-eyes stood a lady in red—
Bill's truck.

He courted it by killing for it.

Cemetery silence, well, shut my mouth.

The tires peel away like a Florida orange—

then head south.

CAROLINA PINES

After leaving a fourfold
of friends and families
pining over pine boxes—
Trail, Madson, Miglin, and Reese—
Andrew found himself about to embark
on the Carolina pines.

He is Proud Mary.
The media wrapped around his trigger-finger.

With the exception of pausing to steal a license plate
in the Palmetto State—

he keeps rolling down I-95 River.

MIAMI DAUPHIN

Cheap-pink as a trailer-park flamingo,
the Normandy Plaza Hotel served efficiently
as chateau by the sea,
the perfect pit for Andrew to beach his storm—
with weekly rates for his princely keep.

Cunanan lay low,
like a bed bug on the underbelly of a bad mattress,
waiting for his moment to step up
as heir-apparent to a designer's dethroning.

Holding crack-cocaine night court with his fresh minions,
regally dining on corn chips, gulps of pint milk,
the occasional single slice of trend pizza—

he was the flop of the flophouse

saying little, soaking little sun

slowly revealing his fleur-de-lies

petal by truck pedal

coming undone.

H-HAZY SHADE OF BUM-SUMMER

Crime. Crime. Crime.
Sea, what's become of Andrew C. or D.?

While he looks around
At his Virtual Monstrosity.

That bitch was so hard to please.

Gaze around.
Biceps are brown.

Manly thighs are a hazy shade of bummer.

Hear the castles crumble in sand.

Down by the Oceanside,
There's bound to be a better bride
Than that bouquet of bullet residue
In your hand.

Carry a fake ID in your wallet, wanted man.

Look around. Latinos are the Miami heat and sound.
And the sky is an FBI helicopter.

Check into a by-the-week rental and flopper.

Hang on to your dope, friend.

That's a sleazy thing to say
When July is here but summer is still
So far away
Like a Carole King hit.
But why bring in that 70s shit?

Crook around for a pawn price.
It's the last line…
of crack or crap in your li(f)e.

I-INCHES AWAY FROM THE PHILIPPINES

Let's face it.
Even with his face pasted
on post-office walls throughout America,
Cunanan was just inches away from the Philippines—

the breakthrough phone call,
an underground connection,
attention-deficit disorder run amuck
at an airline terminal or shipyard—

and bad ol' Guns-and-Hoses was on his Pacific Islander way.

The cad knew how to doctor a fake ID
like applying a band-aid on a pickled knee.

Or perhaps Andrew was another kind of inches away—
a favor fuck or magnificent screw,
one last fabulous daddy before he tailed—ocean blue.

Criminology experts aside,
at that point, it seemed
AC-DC (Andrew Cunanan-Death Chair)
could not quite wield passport and penis together.

Instead,
the ex-gigolo-on-the-go,
half-Filipino, full cold-blooded felon was left
cash-strapped on an infested mattress
with back fashion and gay porn issues
of *Vanity Fair* and *Inches*
strung out, like his mind, among the bedding,

cover models and glossy studs
backlit by the big orange in the sky
peering through the hotel's lint-laden curtains,
a citrus-sphere rising
for each-of-a-peach Floridian,

V-VERSACE. VERSACE. VERSACE.

Being a murder victim along the Cunanan spree
was like being Farrah Fawcett the day Michael Jackson died.

Most of the media hype and national attention
pressing the travel-bag tragedy passed them by
in a South Beach minute—

except for Gianni Versace.

Ah, Versace!

Murder suspect to manhunt,
Andrew's bloodbath a la carte
with newspaper and morning coffee
on the crimson-soaked steps of Casa Casuarina
drew a frenzy of flies with a deadline.

Trail, Madson, even Miglin, and especially Reese
collectively became the middle child of the Bloody Bunch mania—
a Jan Brady in an unseemly black wig, if you will.

And Versace was Marcia! Marcia! Marcia!
All talk, all tabloids!

Andrew designed himself a different kind of killer,
a changed fanatic—omnipresent as oxygen.

Gore had entwined with glamour on the crest of summer.

Cunanan served cold dishes. Versace was death *de jure*.

The others struggled, posthumously, to be remembered—beyond tally.

It is as if they shadow-dashed away with the one most wanted down Ocean Court alley.

NEWS CAFÉ

Ocean Drive was not a runway ritual,
no private stroll, no usual morning saunter
before for the name-call, tell-tale demands
of fame seized my remaining hours.

This was an atypical exercise, magnificent stride.

The weather was postcard-pitch;
the day, a pert, mint-coin model.
Art Deco was drinking its juice for breakfast.

It was the ides of July, inviting sunrise
sent me out of the wrought-iron gate
to fetch my print and pouring.

Otherwise, my good man Arthur would errand.

The inquiries to my last meal
rivaled Jesus and his befuddled disciples.

Coffee appalled,
so, at best, a twist of citrus in bottled water,
and a hoist-haul of papers from the *Herald* to the *Times*,
conventional drag of magazines
nothing for Lady Madonna to muse, da Vinci to paint.

I carried all like a pittance poet with strapless satchel
to beloved Casa Casuarina.

The key extended like a magnet-habit to its home-lock.
A mourning dove descended from a blinding line.
I surmised it might alight on my brow. I heard a cry.

Someone spoke *Versace* to the back of my brain.

My sandals shot forth from indifferent steps like shuffled wings.
And so fashion fell and fashion's king.

An opportunist tourist sopped my blood with pages torn out of *Vogue*.
Family and fans, in time, outraged he had the bladder to tuck and take them.

A rococo in ruins, my dark and deadening eyes read the staining headlines,
                                                    scattered askew,   step-side.
Who knew, the next morning, I myself would make them?

FAGICIDE

If you're a linguist,
a grammarian of any kind,
you'll recognize the word
as a blend, a *portmanteau*,
to be exact—

of, you guessed it,
faggot and *suicide*.

Or perhaps it's a cross
between fudge sicle
and here comes the flagellating queer guide.

Whatever the language ménage-a-trois,
it's less mess,

not so much for the pancake-selling press,

but for the dapper-vested

FBI.

HE COULD'VE BEEN ANYTHING

That is the select phrase
the narrator on *Biography Channel*
uses to open and close
The Andrew Cunanan Show.

This choice of words,
this parlance, as it were,
may have referred
to the young man's
soaring IQ
or his chameleon-like charisma
that changed with the company kept,
brash club where he stepped,
or the person at any crash moment
with whom he disco-nap slept.

The line is twice spoken
with a tone of might-have-been shucks,
a touch of sardonic media wit.

Images of Andrew as head surgeon,
estate attorney, revered anthropologist
rise to the viewer's mind,
then abruptly dismissed.

He could have been anything—
as if to imply he had been nothing—

from a murderous wielder of a claw hammer
to felonious transgressor of decency and law.

There is nothing like anything,
and he was.

He was.

THE BEHEADING OF JOHN THE BAPTIST

Several fortnights after turning Lee Miglin into a human jigsaw,
the remains of Andrew Cunanan bides in San Diego.

His mother, MaryAnn, arranges for her deceased son
to be part of a Mass for the Souls interred a week earlier at Holy Cross.

It is August 29th,
a day chosen in the Roman Catholic Church
to commemorate the beheading of John the Baptist.

It is proven in *Matthew*.
It is printed in *Mark*.
It is spoken as feasting scripture this day by the priest of the ceremony
among the dozens of downed heads
who had no idea they were to mourn the infamous this Friday.

Caravaggio painted a frame of the Biblical decollation—
Salome, the Executioner, and the cousin of Jesus—
his head on a plate.

Mother MaryAnn walks among the praying, the disbelieving.
Her palm reaches in a dark pocket to reveal mass cards in Andrew's name.

A most unexpected offering,
the congregation seems apprehensive to accept this last letter, final epistle.

In testament, in tandem,
the priest speaks of John's severed neck.

Images of Miglin's slit throat commence to resurrect.
Images cut to the brief
by a diabolical harp, a garden bow saw.

It is an hour for the books. It is an hour for the holy and the horror hereafter.

On the reverse side of Cunanan's memory bill,
his mother has paid to print—
he be remembered in happiness and laughter.

THE ONLY LIVING BOY ON THE HOUSEBOAT

Somewhere between a John Updike novel
and a Simon and Garfunkel song,
there lies Andrew Cunanan.

He is *Rabbit at Rest*.
He is the only living boy on the houseboat.

And like that Rabbit character,
he has chosen to repose in a Florida hideaway,
alien to his own soul, dredging for reasons to live.

A sponge on the ocean,
absorbing last assets from the vacated owner,
Cunanan occupies residences like he occupies the American mind.

Once he breaks into the floating premises,
South Beach Police report—
the savage by the sea lives like a slob. In cold defiance—
he picks the door lock, places it in a butter dish, inside the ice box.

He uses the upstairs bathtub as a repository for waste,
discarded papers front-paging his terror,
bloodied cotton balls from a stomach wound.

The once posh-and-pristine Prince of the Southern California gay scene
lets himself go to seed.

His final target is his first target: himself.

Officials find him among a down sail of soiled sheets,
a flotsam of strewn soda cans, victim of self-infliction, suicide by land and by sea.

A boy born, in all places, National City,
now harbors a nation's anger, relief, and perhaps its pity.
Even in death, he gathers all the news about him –like a weather report.
Lying in a loveless loveseat, his corpse is more a chorus of confessions
echoing from silent chambers—speaking nothing of motive, reason, or plan.

Three words, at best, all the FBI, the world will get—not a syllable of regret—three words:

Here I am.

ABOUT THE AUTHOR

John David Thompson is the author
of 12 books, 11 of them poetry, including
Titanic: A Centenarian Voyage of Verse and
Fame on You: 50 Shameless Ways to Make You Famous.
The poet lives and teaches in Iowa and
may be reached at the following e-mail.

statepoetpro@yahoo.com

www.ingramcontent.com/pod-product-compliance
Lightning Source LLC
Chambersburg PA
CBHW081521040426

42447CB00013B/3293

* 9 7 8 0 9 7 2 0 7 1 7 7 2 *